AF599211

Adapted by
Kathleen Hanrahan

Published by Sequoia Kids Media,
an imprint of Sequoia Publishing & Media, LLC

Sequoia Publishing & Media, LLC,
a division of Phoenix International Publications, Inc.

8501 West Higgins Road, Chicago, Illinois 60631
34 Seymour Street, London W1H 7JE
Heimhuder Straße 81, 20148 Hamburg

CustomerService@PhoenixInternational.com

www.SequoiaKidsMedia.com

Library of Congress Control Number: 2024931778

ISBN: 979-8-7654-0339-6

active★minds

YOU can draw CRETACEOUS DINOSAURS

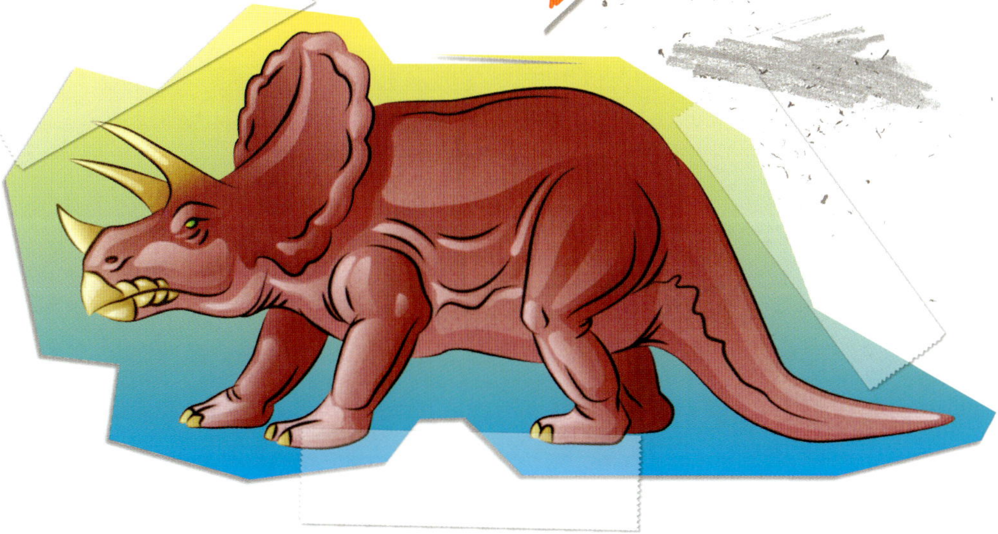

Written and illustrated by
JAMES MRAVEC

An imprint of PHOENIX International Publications, Inc.

USING THIS BOOK

Drawing is fun and not as hard as you may think! One of the trade secrets is that any object can be broken down into smaller parts. The step-by-step instructions in this book show you how to use this secret to draw some prehistoric favorites. You can use the skills you learn to draw anything else!

Drawing requires some basic tools. Make sure you have a pencil, an eraser, a pen or marker, and—of course—the grid paper where you'll make your drawings. To print this grid paper, visit **SEQUOIAKIDSMEDIA.COM/BONUS-CONTENT.**

The sketches in this book start with basic shapes. Using a pencil, lightly draw the full shape, even if some of it will not be seen in the final drawing—you'll erase those parts later! Keeping the lines light until you are happy with their placement will make them easier to erase. Each step adds more detail to the drawing. The red lines show what to draw in each step, while the gray lines show the lines drawn in previous steps.

Each drawing is shown on a grid to help you copy the image. While you draw, look closely at how the lines and shapes fit on the grid—watch where the drawn lines come close to the grid lines and where they cross over them. Try to copy the drawn lines exactly on your grid paper.

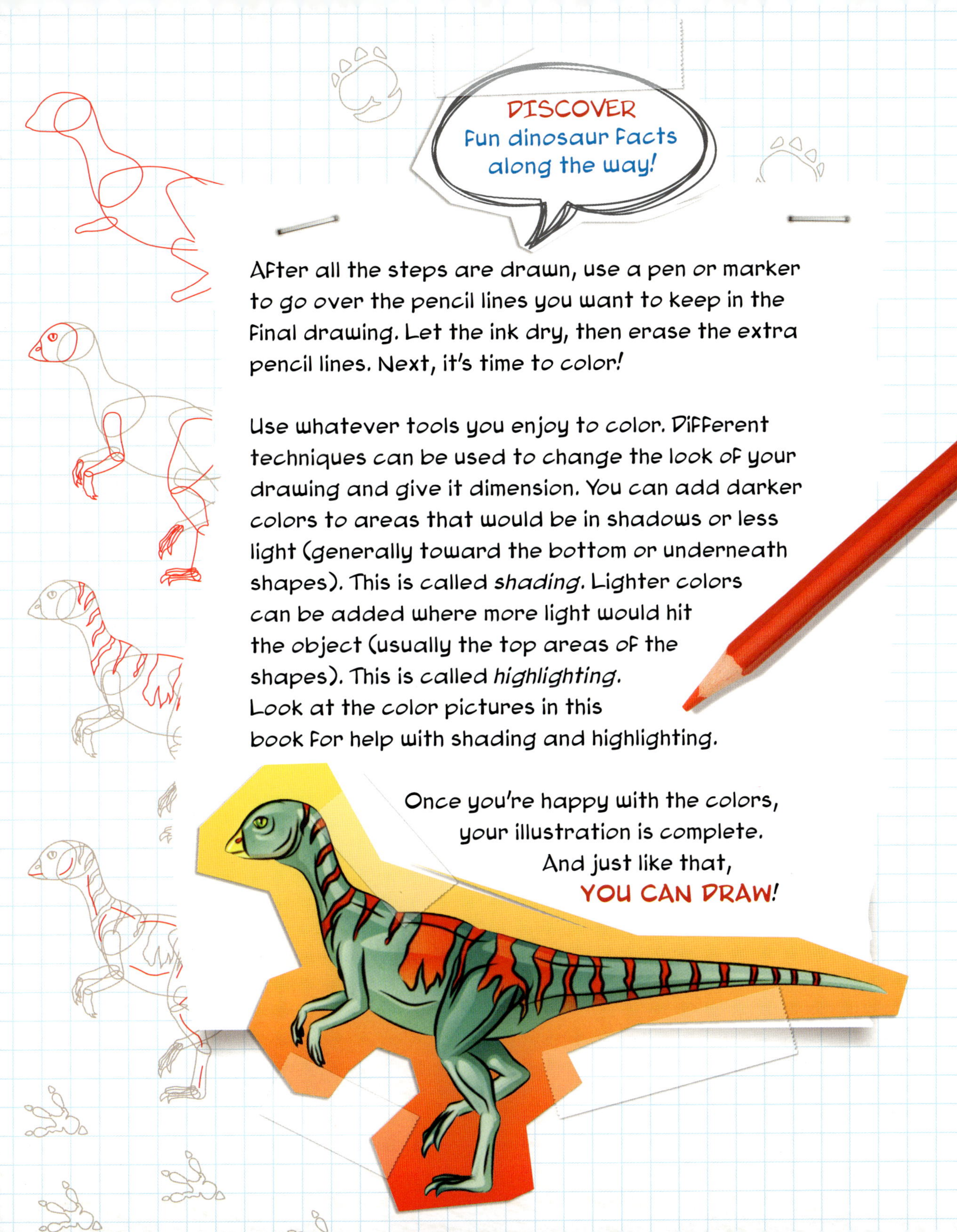

After all the steps are drawn, use a pen or marker to go over the pencil lines you want to keep in the final drawing. Let the ink dry, then erase the extra pencil lines. Next, it's time to color!

Use whatever tools you enjoy to color. Different techniques can be used to change the look of your drawing and give it dimension. You can add darker colors to areas that would be in shadows or less light (generally toward the bottom or underneath shapes). This is called *shading*. Lighter colors can be added where more light would hit the object (usually the top areas of the shapes). This is called *highlighting*. Look at the color pictures in this book for help with shading and highlighting.

Once you're happy with the colors, your illustration is complete. And just like that, **YOU CAN DRAW!**

ANKYLOSAURUS

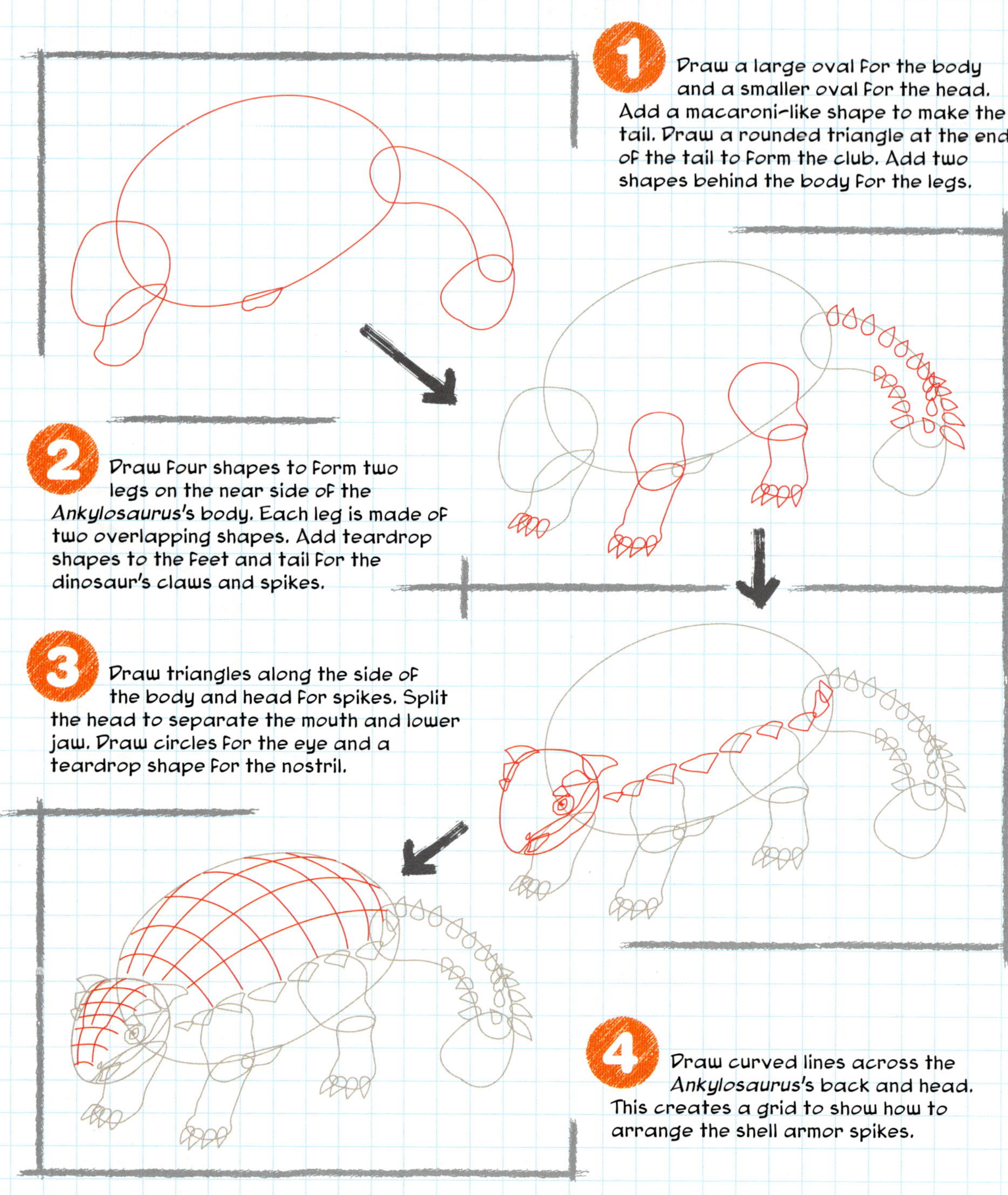

1 Draw a large oval for the body and a smaller oval for the head. Add a macaroni-like shape to make the tail. Draw a rounded triangle at the end of the tail to form the club. Add two shapes behind the body for the legs.

2 Draw four shapes to form two legs on the near side of the *Ankylosaurus*'s body. Each leg is made of two overlapping shapes. Add teardrop shapes to the feet and tail for the dinosaur's claws and spikes.

3 Draw triangles along the side of the body and head for spikes. Split the head to separate the mouth and lower jaw. Draw circles for the eye and a teardrop shape for the nostril.

4 Draw curved lines across the *Ankylosaurus*'s back and head. This creates a grid to show how to arrange the shell armor spikes.

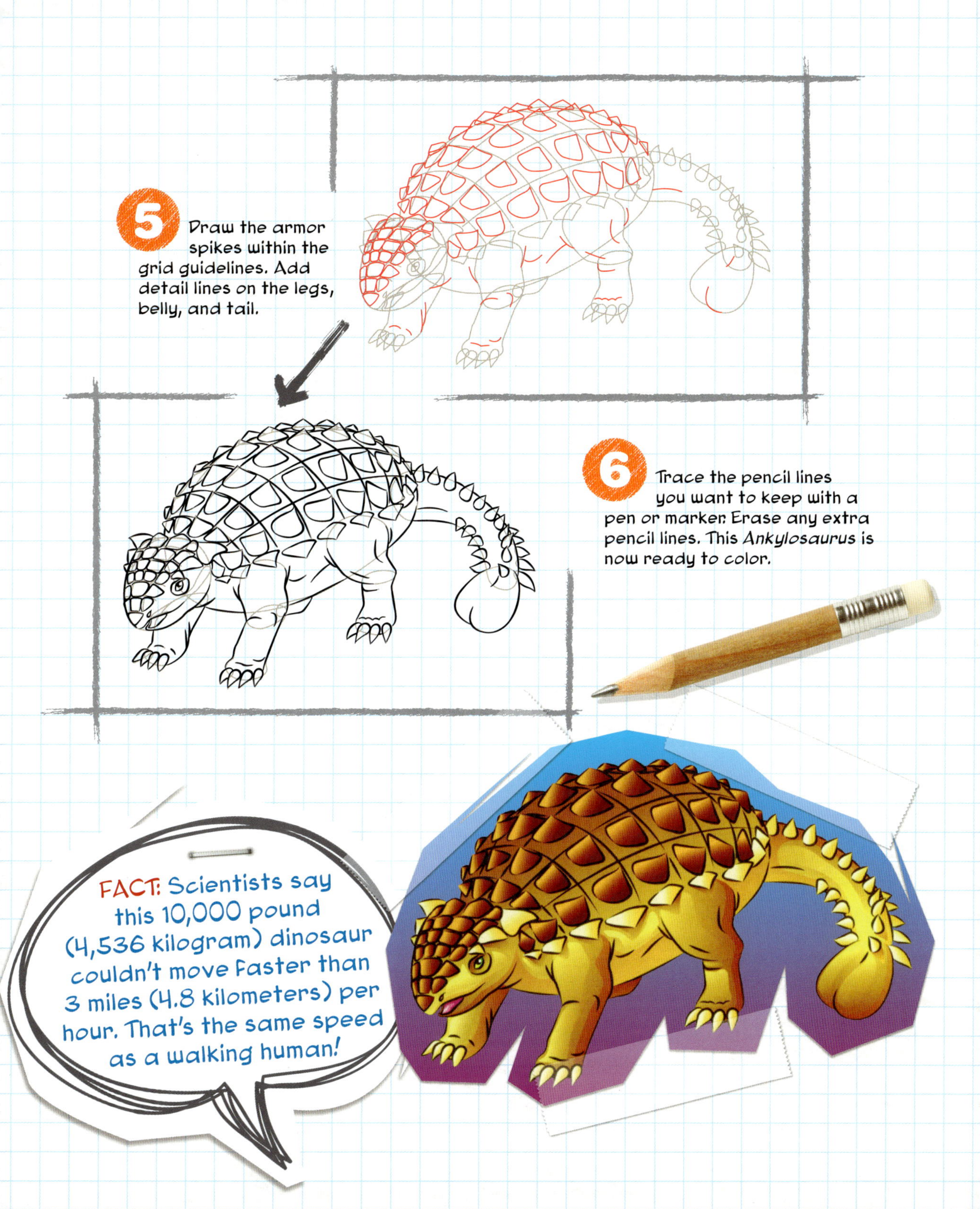
5
Draw the armor spikes within the grid guidelines. Add detail lines on the legs, belly, and tail.
6
Trace the pencil lines you want to keep with a pen or marker. Erase any extra pencil lines. This *Ankylosaurus* is now ready to color.
FACT: Scientists say this 10,000 pound (4,536 kilogram) dinosaur couldn't move faster than 3 miles (4.8 kilometers) per hour. That's the same speed as a walking human!

HYPSILOPHODON

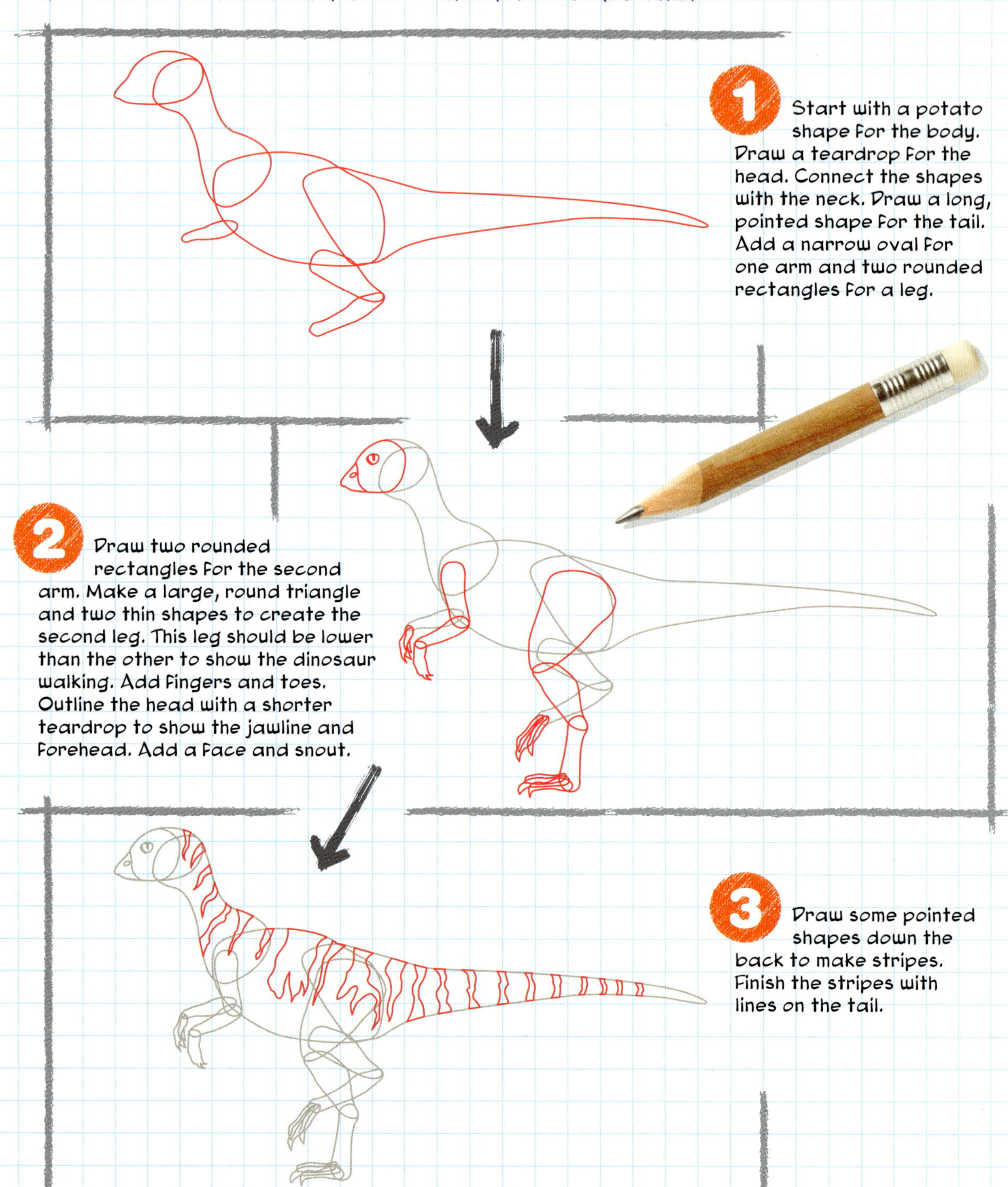

1 Start with a potato shape for the body. Draw a teardrop for the head. Connect the shapes with the neck. Draw a long, pointed shape for the tail. Add a narrow oval for one arm and two rounded rectangles for a leg.

2 Draw two rounded rectangles for the second arm. Make a large, round triangle and two thin shapes to create the second leg. This leg should be lower than the other to show the dinosaur walking. Add fingers and toes. Outline the head with a shorter teardrop to show the jawline and forehead. Add a face and snout.

3 Draw some pointed shapes down the back to make stripes. Finish the stripes with lines on the tail.

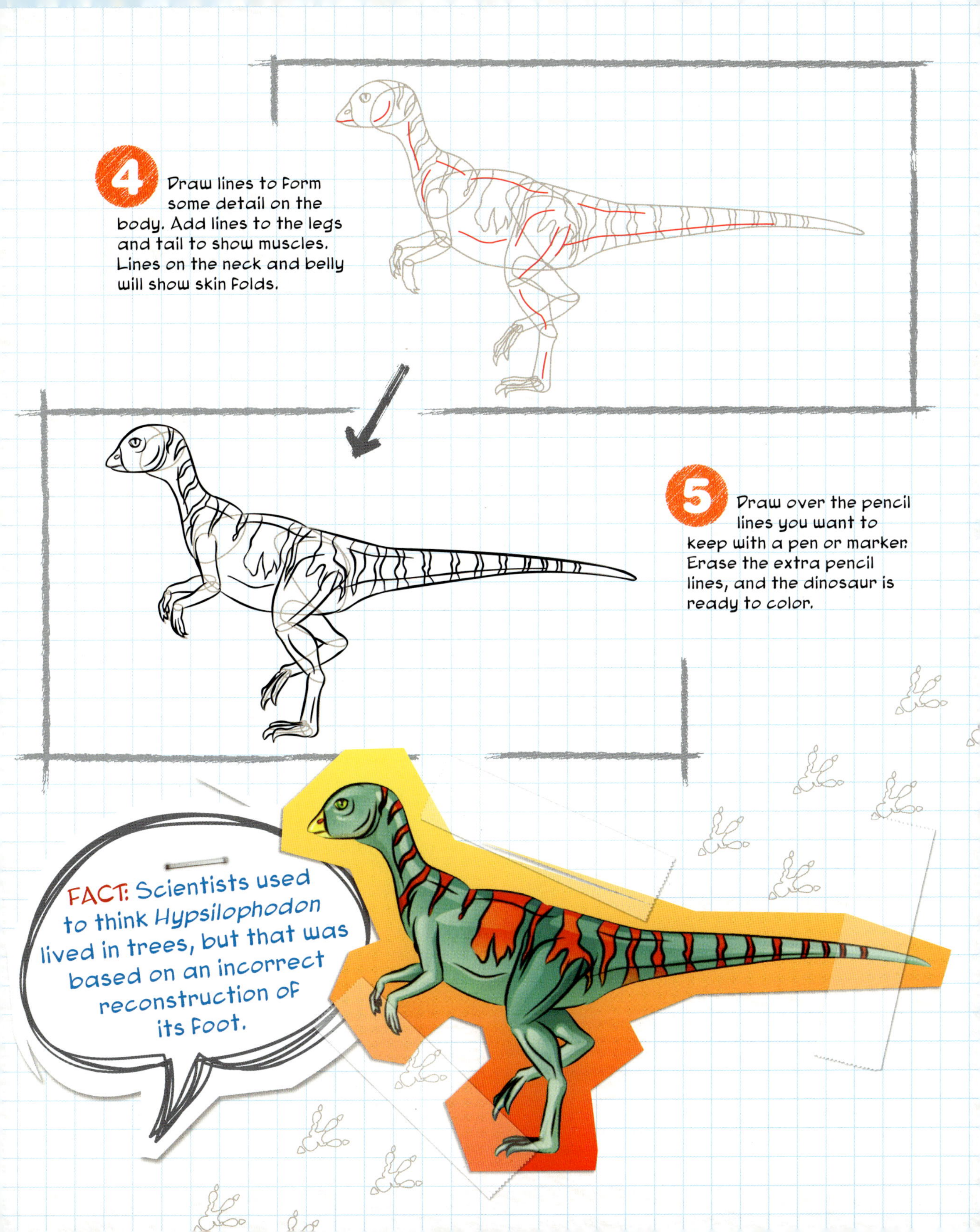
4
Draw lines to form some detail on the body. Add lines to the legs and tail to show muscles. Lines on the neck and belly will show skin folds.
5
Draw over the pencil lines you want to keep with a pen or marker. Erase the extra pencil lines, and the dinosaur is ready to color.
FACT: Scientists used to think *Hypsilophodon* lived in trees, but that was based on an incorrect reconstruction of its foot.

OVIRAPTOR

1 Start with two potato shapes—a large one for the body and a smaller one for the head. Connect the two shapes with another curved shape to form the neck.

2 Draw a curved, pointed tail. Split the head into two shapes for the upper and lower jaws. Add a triangle on top of the head for the crest. Create the leg on the near side of the body using three shapes. The leg on the far side will be partially hidden, so that will only use two shapes.

3 Draw one shape for the arm on the far side and two for the arm on the near side. Add a crescent inside of a circle for the eye. Add a circle for the ear and a teardrop for the nostril. Draw a mitten shape for the beak and a tongue in the mouth. Add details to the rest of the mouth.

4 Make hooks at the end of each arm for the fingers and claws. Add three longer spike shapes at the end of each foot for more claws. Be sure to include a fourth claw on the back of the far foot.

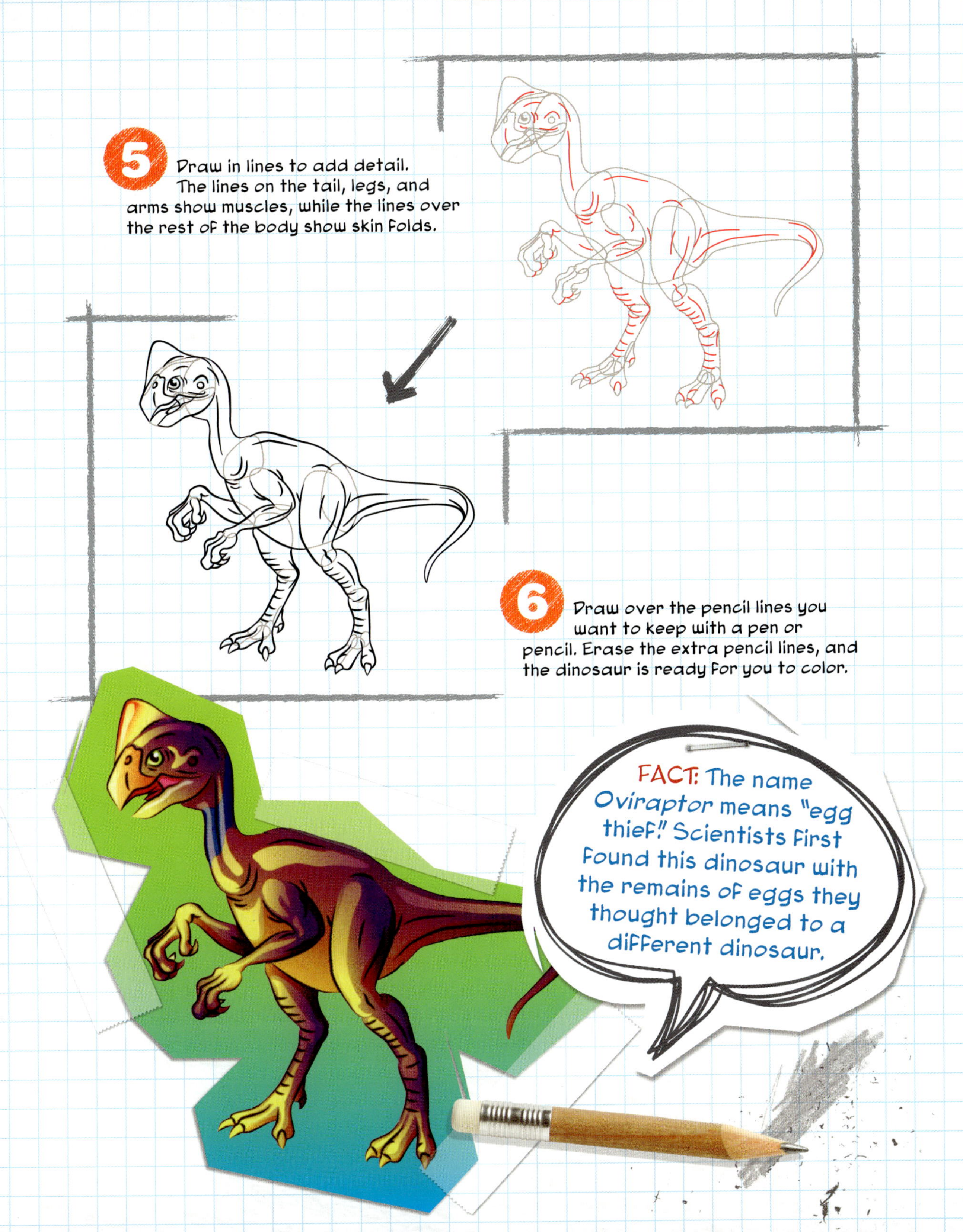
5
Draw in lines to add detail. The lines on the tail, legs, and arms show muscles, while the lines over the rest of the body show skin folds.
6
Draw over the pencil lines you want to keep with a pen or pencil. Erase the extra pencil lines, and the dinosaur is ready for you to color.
FACT: The name Oviraptor means "egg thief." Scientists first found this dinosaur with the remains of eggs they thought belonged to a different dinosaur.

PACHYCEPHALOSAURUS

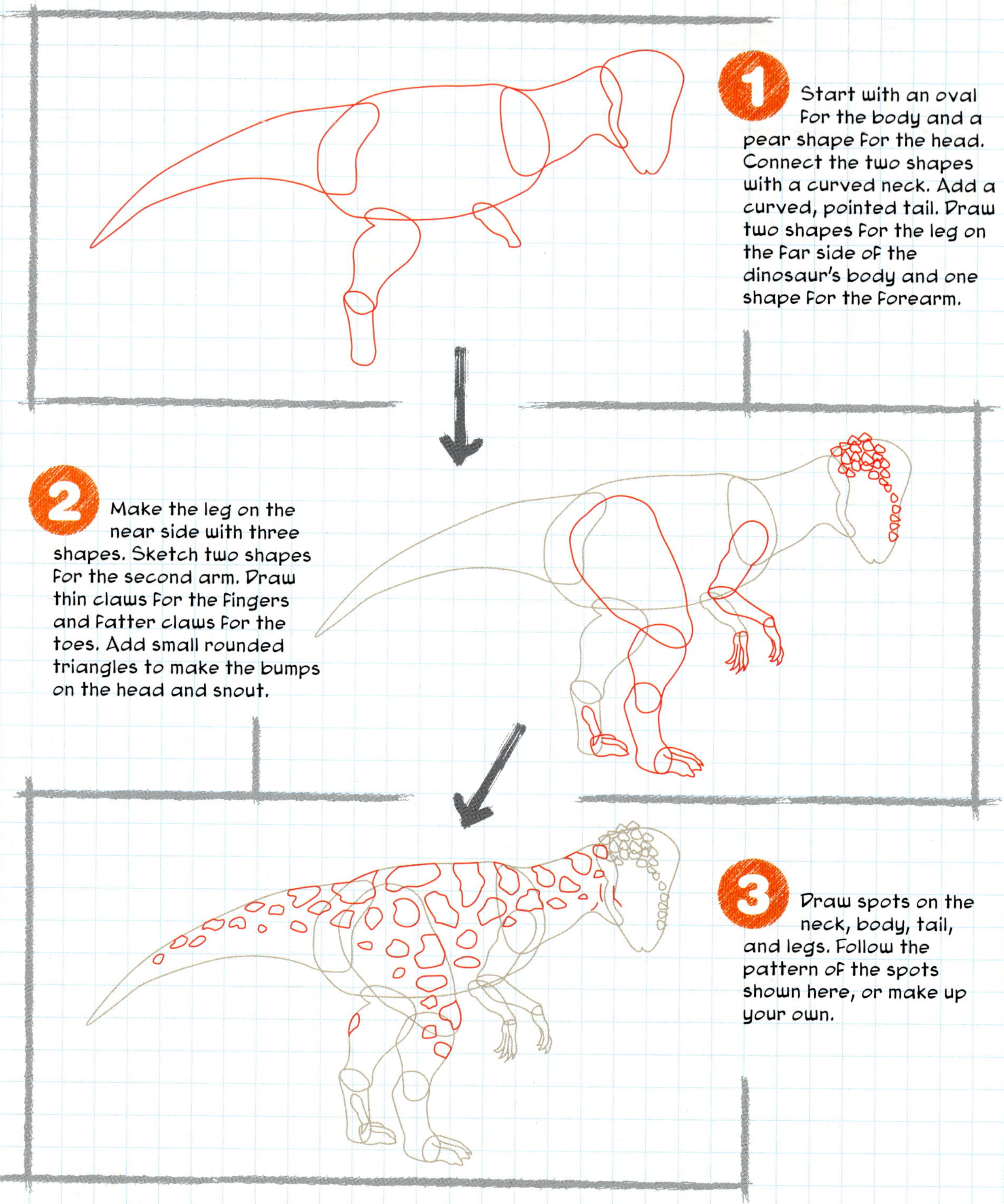

1 Start with an oval for the body and a pear shape for the head. Connect the two shapes with a curved neck. Add a curved, pointed tail. Draw two shapes for the leg on the far side of the dinosaur's body and one shape for the forearm.

2 Make the leg on the near side with three shapes. Sketch two shapes for the second arm. Draw thin claws for the fingers and fatter claws for the toes. Add small rounded triangles to make the bumps on the head and snout.

3 Draw spots on the neck, body, tail, and legs. Follow the pattern of the spots shown here, or make up your own.

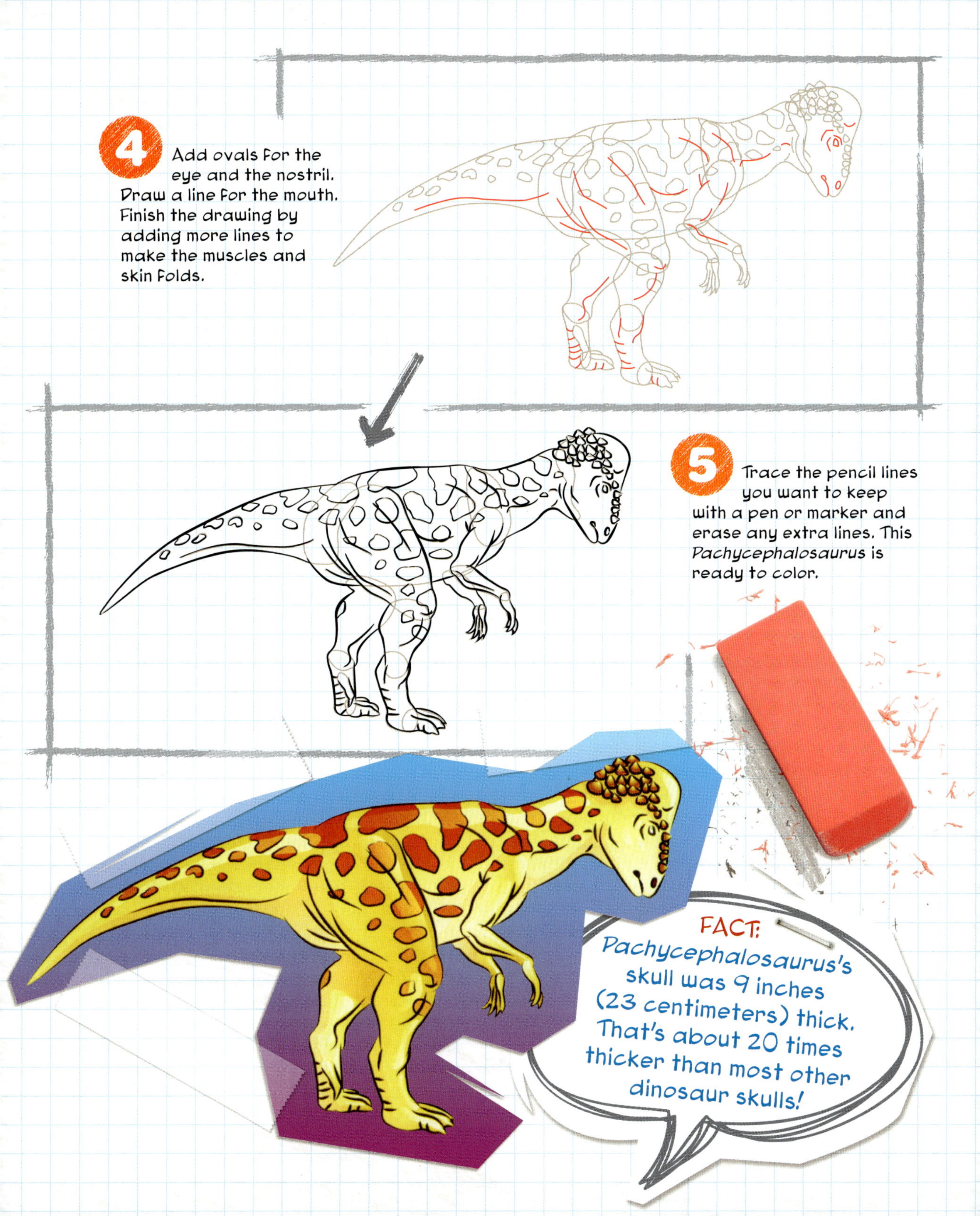
4
Add ovals for the eye and the nostril. Draw a line for the mouth. Finish the drawing by adding more lines to make the muscles and skin folds.
5
Trace the pencil lines you want to keep with a pen or marker and erase any extra lines. This *Pachycephalosaurus* is ready to color.
FACT:
Pachycephalosaurus's skull was 9 inches (23 centimeters) thick. That's about 20 times thicker than most other dinosaur skulls!

QUETZALCOATLUS

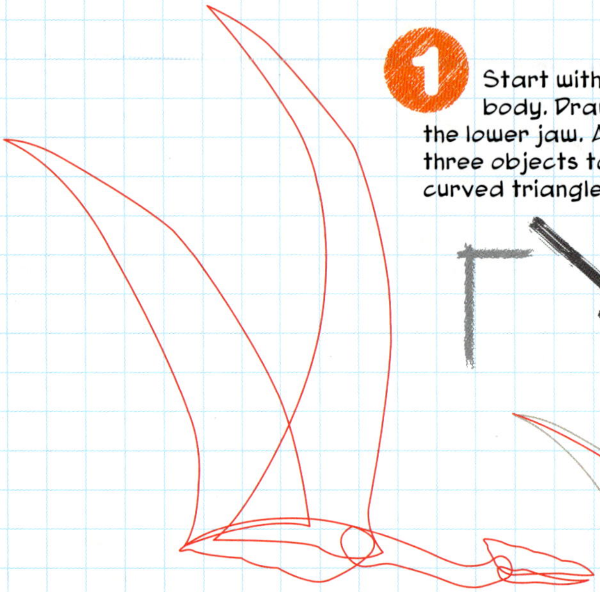

1 Start with a teardrop on its side for the body. Draw two triangles for the head and the lower jaw. Add a curved shape between the three objects to make the neck. Draw two long, curved triangles for the wings.

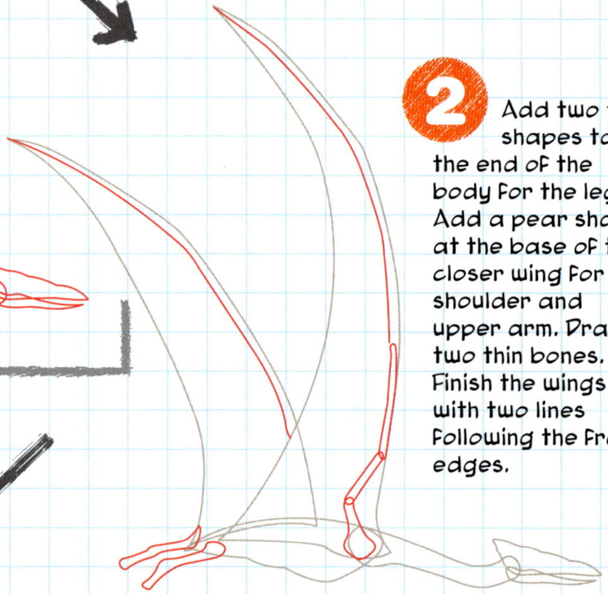

2 Add two thin shapes to the end of the body for the legs. Add a pear shape at the base of the closer wing for the shoulder and upper arm. Draw two thin bones. Finish the wings with two lines following the front edges.

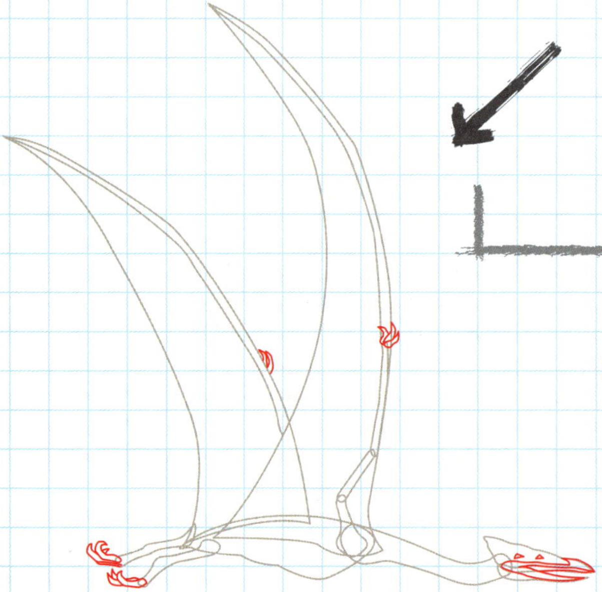

3 Draw claws about halfway up each wing and to each foot. Sketch small triangles for the eyes and nostril. Add a triangle for the beak, and finish the mouth with some lines for detail.

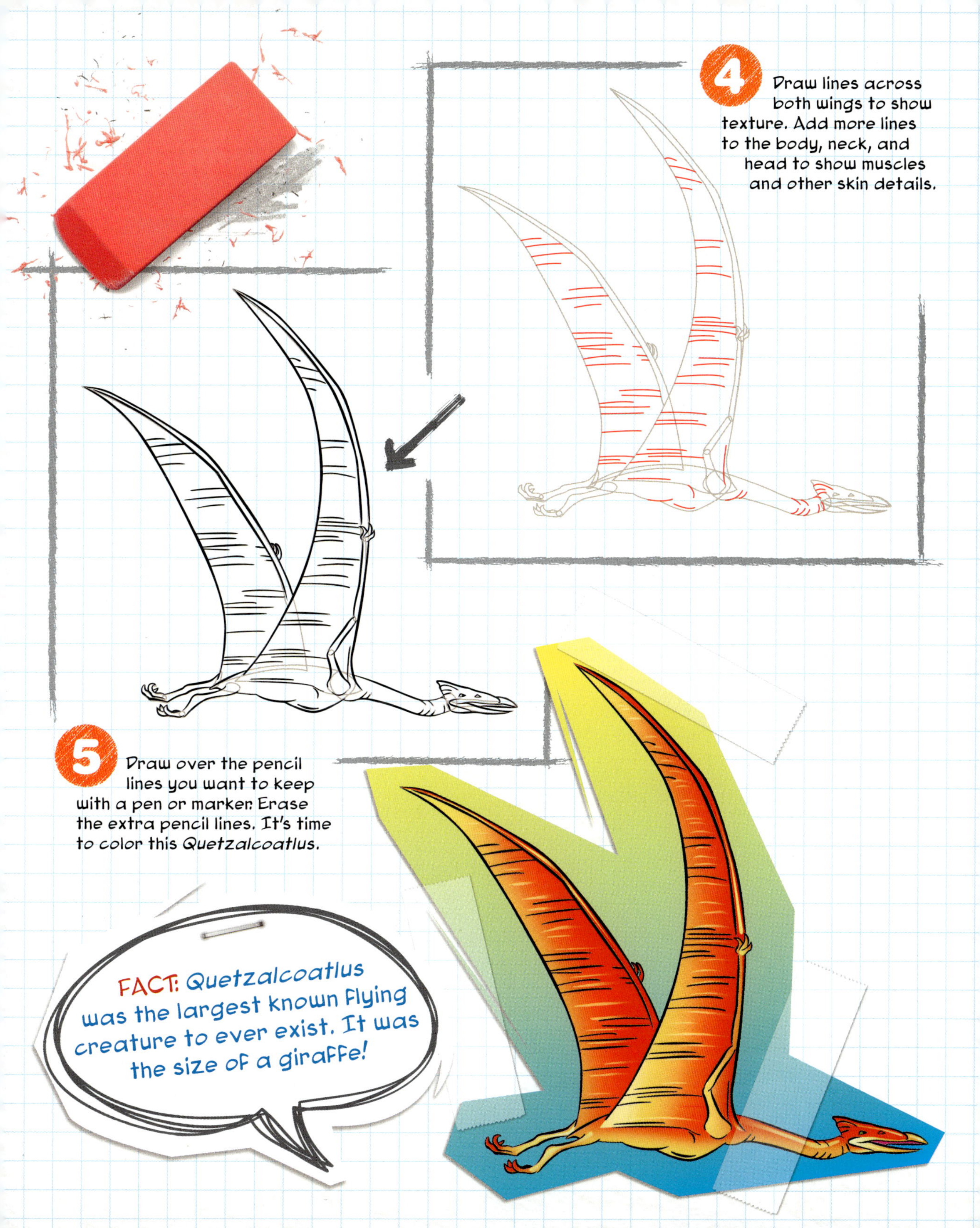
4
Draw lines across both wings to show texture. Add more lines to the body, neck, and head to show muscles and other skin details.
5
Draw over the pencil lines you want to keep with a pen or marker. Erase the extra pencil lines. It's time to color this *Quetzalcoatlus*.
FACT: *Quetzalcoatlus* was the largest known flying creature to ever exist. It was the size of a giraffe!

TRICERATOPS

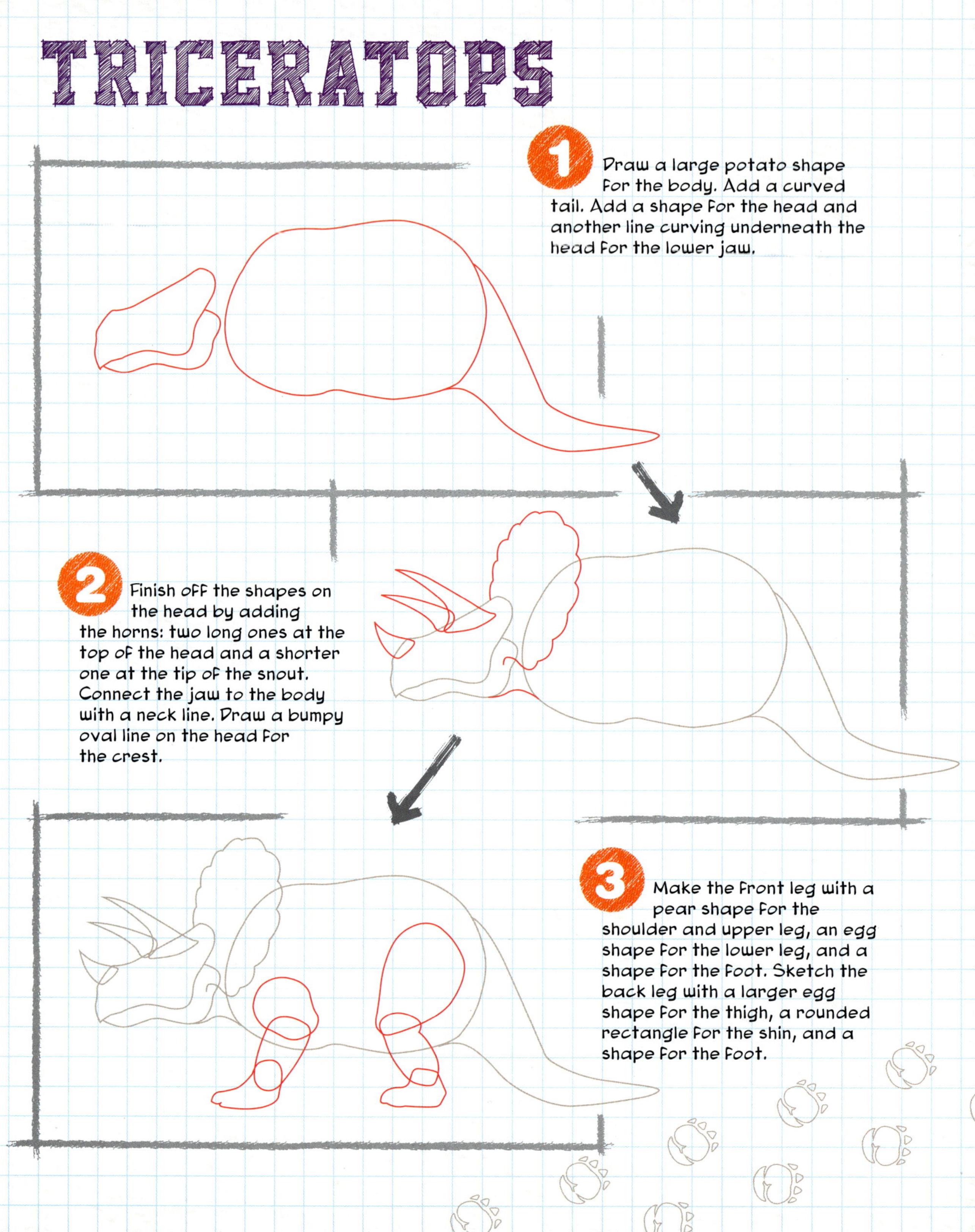

1 Draw a large potato shape for the body. Add a curved tail. Add a shape for the head and another line curving underneath the head for the lower jaw.

2 Finish off the shapes on the head by adding the horns: two long ones at the top of the head and a shorter one at the tip of the snout. Connect the jaw to the body with a neck line. Draw a bumpy oval line on the head for the crest.

3 Make the front leg with a pear shape for the shoulder and upper leg, an egg shape for the lower leg, and a shape for the foot. Sketch the back leg with a larger egg shape for the thigh, a rounded rectangle for the shin, and a shape for the foot.

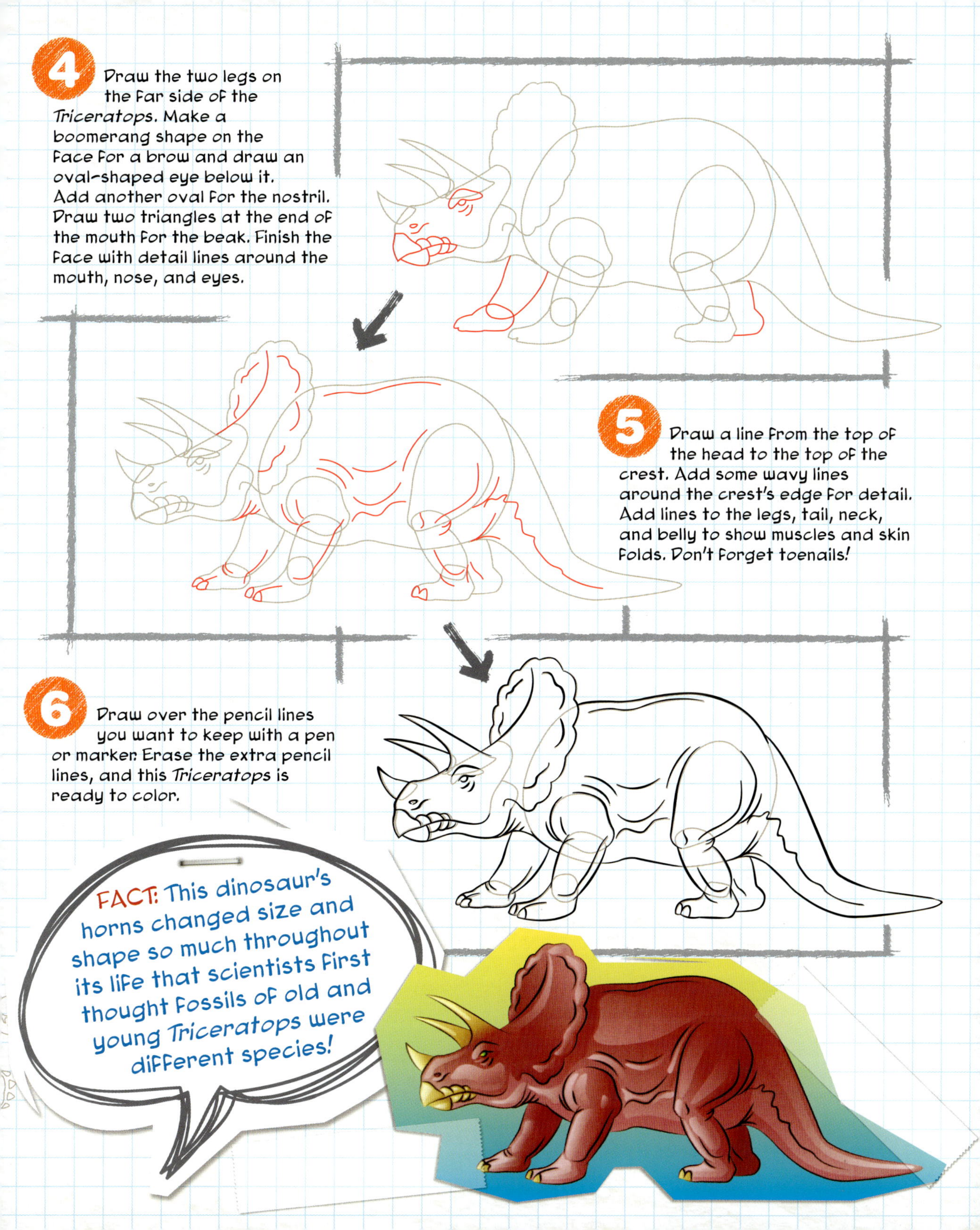
4
Draw the two legs on the far side of the *Triceratops*. Make a boomerang shape on the face for a brow and draw an oval-shaped eye below it. Add another oval for the nostril. Draw two triangles at the end of the mouth for the beak. Finish the face with detail lines around the mouth, nose, and eyes.
5
Draw a line from the top of the head to the top of the crest. Add some wavy lines around the crest's edge for detail. Add lines to the legs, tail, neck, and belly to show muscles and skin folds. Don't forget toenails!
6
Draw over the pencil lines you want to keep with a pen or marker. Erase the extra pencil lines, and this *Triceratops* is ready to color.
FACT: This dinosaur's horns changed size and shape so much throughout its life that scientists first thought fossils of old and young *Triceratops* were different species!

CREATE A SCENE

Below are some elements that could be found in these dinosaurs' habitats. Using these elements—and your imagination—create a scene with some of the dinosaurs you just learned to draw. Look at the examples on the next page for inspiration.

Quetzalcoatlus

Ankylosaurus

Pachycephalosaurus

Triceratops

Hypsilophodon

Oviraptor